WISDOM TREE

Contents

1. **Patriotism**   3
   Ask not what your country can do for you, ask what you can do for your country

2. **Honesty**   9
   Honesty is the best policy

4. **Respect for the Elderly**   15
   Respect your elders; be a better listener than a talker

5. **Sincerity**   23
   It pays to be sincere

   Moral Crossword   31

6. **Non-Violence**   32
   An eye for an eye will make the world blind

7. **Loyalty**   40
   You give loyalty, you get it back

   A Test of Your Values   46

   Values for You   48

Patriotism

How do you feel when your country's cricket team wins a match? Do you feel proud when the national anthem is being played? Do you like it when people from other countries enjoy the local food of your country? If you do, you are patriotic.

Showing one's love and support for one's country is patriotism. Patriotism is not just loving one's country. It is loving one's country very strongly.

Let us know more about the value through the following story about India.

The Story

In November 2008, terrorists had attacked the city of Mumbai. They were on the streets, at railway stations and even at one of the star hotels, a prominent landmark in the city.

Some terrorists had entered the 100-year-old Taj Mahal Palace Hotel in Mumbai. They held several of the guests as hostages. Everyone feared for the lives of these guests.

In the meantime, the Indian army was deployed to save the people of Mumbai and capture the terrorists.

Major Sandeep Unnikrishnan was one of those army personnel sent into the hotel to save the guests and capture the terrorists. It was the start of the Operation Black Tornado. He along with nine other commandos traced some terrorists on the third floor of the hotel. Suspecting the terrorists to be holding hostages there, they made their way carefully to the locked door. The terrorists and some women were behind that door.

The commandos broke open the door and a round of fire ensued. One of Unnikrishnan's colleagues got hurt in that fight. Unnikrishnan chased the terrorists, who were running away from there. In the fight that followed, he was shot from the back and he sadly died.

Such was his bravery and dedication to his country that he died trying to protect some of his fellow countrymen.

About Major Unnikrishnan: He was born in 1977 and died for the country at the age of 31. He grew up in the city of Bengaluru and had always been interested in being a part of the Indian army. He was a part of several operations for the country, including the Operation Black Tornado, in which he gave up his life for our country. He was awarded the Ashoka Chakra for his bravery and service to the nation.

Have you understood the story? Answer the following questions.

1. Why did some Indian army personnel enter the famous Taj Mahal Palace Hotel in Mumbai in November 2008?

2. At what other places did the terrorists strike that evening?

3. Name one army personnel who was part of the Operation Black Tornado.

4. Why was the Major awarded the Ashoka Chakra?

5. How did the Major show his love for his country?

_____
_____
_____

More about the Value

Patriotism is not just about dying for one's country. It is not even merely fighting and going to war for it. When the need arises, patriotic people do fight or die for their country.

But patriotism is loving one's country, being proud of it and all its culture and people.

Why do we need patriotism? Patriotism is a good value. We have to learn to love and respect what is our own. Don't we love our family? Even though your brother might tease you, or your parents might not allow you to play video games, you love them. You help them, and protect them. You feel proud when they achieve something. When they go wrong, you correct them. Such should be our love not just for our family, but also for our country, its people and its culture.

Just as we do not harm our family members, we should not harm our fellow countrymen. Just as we help our family when in need, we should also help our fellow countrymen when they are in need.

When you have this kind of a feeling for your country and countrymen, you are patriotic.

A VALUE FOR ME

Ask not what your country can do for you; ask what you can do for your country.

Snippet

When Gandhiji was living in South Africa, he was awarded a number of medals by the British government for his various services.

However, later in life, when Gandhiji realized that his countrymen in the Indian subcontinent were suffering under the British rule, he returned all his medals to the British.

This was his way of showing patriotism.

Let Us Do

1. **How much do you know about India? Now answer the following and solve the puzzle.**

   Across:
   2. The number of spokes on the Ashoka Chakra is twenty-_____.
   4. _____ is another name for India.
   5. The Indian national bird is _____.
   6. He is considered the Father of the Nation: _____
   8. India is surrounded by two seas and _____ oceans.

   Down:
   1. India became independent on 15th August from the _____.
   2. Another country that ruled parts of India. _____
   3. Before New Delhi, the British ruled India from this city. _____
   5. The Indian Independence Day speech is delivered by the _____.
   7. _____ is India's national sport.

2. **Rearrange the letters to form meaningful words, which are all related to India.**

   a. TLRICROUO   _____

   b. GLFA   _____

   c. ANHIGDIJ   _____

   d. DREORFT   _____

   e. FOREDEM   _____

   f. BTARHA   _____

   g. PRADAE   _____

   h. INEPEDDENCEN   _____

   i. AASOKH CAKRAH   _____

3. **Make a collage of all things of your country that you like. But first, list out the things here and also write why you like them.**

   _____
   _____
   _____
   _____
   _____
   _____
   _____
   _____
   _____
   _____

4. **Write at least three things about your country that makes it different from any other country in the world.**

   _____
   _____
   _____
   _____
   _____
   _____

Stick pictures in the following space to explain your answer.

_____	_____	_____

Are you a patriotic person?

a. Do you stand in attention whenever the national anthem it is played?

b. Do you like it when you hear negative news about your country?

c. Do you know any national integration songs? Name any two.

_____   _____

d. Do you know your national symbols? Name any two. Draw them too.

_____   _____

e. Do you love the culture of your country?

If your answer to all these questions has been a 'yes' and you have been able to fill up the blanks, you are a patriotic person.

Tips to Parents and Teachers

Speak good things about the country. Tell them about the strengths of the country. Rather than merely pointing out the negative aspects that trouble our country, try to discuss with children on how to tackle such issues.

Make the discussions participatory and welcome their ideas as well. If possible, help them in implementing their ideas at community level.

Do's and Don'ts

1. Stand in attention whenever the national anthem is being played.

2. Don't belittle our country. Talk good things about the country.

3. Be thankful for what our country offers us. We have a rich culture and ancient history that very few nations have.

4. Learn to sing the national anthem without any mistakes. Learn its meaning as well.

Honesty

Telling the truth makes you an honest person. When you do things sincerely, you are an honest person. When you don't cheat others, you are an honest person. Honesty is the quality of being honest.

Honest people are loved and respected by others.

The Woodcutter and His Axe

Long ago, a woodcutter ventured deep into the forest in search of good wood to cut. On finding a tree to his satisfaction, he put himself to work.

It so happened that the tree he was felling was right next to a river. While felling the tree, his axe accidentally fell into the river. The woodcutter became miserable. The river was deep and he did not know how to swim.

There was no way he could dive into the river to get back his axe. Buying another axe was out of question because he was very poor and he had no money for it. He broke down into tears.

As he sat on the banks of the river crying, the river goddess appeared before him. Naturally, the woodcutter was stunned to see the goddess. The goddess asked him kindly, "What happened? Why are you crying?"

The woodcutter then told her his plight. After listening to him, the goddess told him not to worry. She went back to the river from which she had appeared. A few minutes later, she reappeared with an axe in her hand.

"Is this your axe?" she asked the woodcutter. The woodcutter was stunned. The axe in the goddess' hand was made of pure gold. "No dear Goddess, this is not my axe. This is made of gold. I am but a poor woodcutter. I cannot afford such an axe," he said truthfully.

The goddess once again disappeared into the river. A few minutes later, she brought a silver axe to the woodcutter. She asked him if that was his axe. Once again, the woodcutter replied in a similar manner. "This is also an expensive axe, Goddess. This is not mine."

The goddess went back into the water for the third time. A couple of minutes later she came out with an iron axe. This time the woodcutter was pleased to see the axe that the goddess held. "Yes, Mother Goddess! This is mine! This is the very one that fell into the river," the woodcutter exclaimed with joy.

So pleased was the goddess with the woodcutter's honesty that she gave the two precious axes as well as the woodcutter's old axe to him. The woodcutter sold the precious axes and got so much of money for them that he no longer had to fell wood for a living.

Have you understood the story? Now answer the following questions.

1. Why was the woodcutter miserable?
   _____
   _____

2. Who appeared out of the river?
   _____
   _____

3. Why did the woodcutter refuse to take the first axe that the goddess brought from the river?
   _____
   _____

4. Do you think the woodcutter was honest? Give reasons for your answer.
   _____
   _____

5. How was the woodcutter rewarded for his honesty?
   _____
   _____

More about the Value

When you have honest people around you, you don't have to think whether the other person is lying or not; you don't have to worry whether the other person is cheating you or not.

These days, we hear the word CORRUPTION very often. Corruption means dishonesty. When people are not honest, they are dishonest or corrupt. It means that people do not do their duty the way they are supposed to. Often people take money or other gifts for completing the work that they ought to do as part of their duty.

Corruption is ruining our world. If everyone in our country is honest, then our country can develop better and become a better place to live in.

A VALUE FOR ME
Honesty is the best policy.

Snippet

Once, a young man named Anil went to St. Stephen's College in Delhi. He was there to deposit an admission fee. It was a hot day, and the queue was very long. After a while, Anil fainted due to the heat. The people nearby took him to the dispensary. When Anil came back to consciousness, the people there asked him who he was and where he lived, so that they could help him get back home. He replied that he was Anil,  son of Lal Bahadur Shastri. The people there were shocked. He was the son of the then Prime Minister of India.

Not taking advantage of positions is also honesty.

Let Us Do

1. **Tick the correct statements below.**

    a. An honest person is one who never lies.

    b. An honest person never obeys laws.

    c. An honest person cheats others for personal benefit.

    d. An honest person does his or her work sincerely.

    e. An honest person is responsible about the work he or she does.

2. **Who among these is an honest person?**

    a. Someone broke the tube light in the classroom. The teacher asked the class, "Who broke the light?" Sally knew who did it. She, however, did not speak up. Is Sally an honest person?

    Yes   No

    b. Mike has a fish tank at home. While his parents were away for a month, they gave him the responsibility of keeping the tank clean and the fish fed. He fed the fish every evening and cleaned the tank once a week. Is Mike an honest person?

    Yes   No

c. The bus passes through the new road every morning. There is hardly anyone on the road. The bus driver never stops at the red light because there are no other vehicles at the junction. Is the bus driver an honest person?

Yes   No

3. How do you think you could become an honest person? Follow these and you can become an honest person.

1. Know when you lie and whom you lie to. Try to avoid lying again, in similar situations.

2. Do only those things that you can do; try not to do things where you will have to lie or cheat to finish the task.

3. Always do things that make you feel proud of yourself.

4. Be happy with what you have.

5. Accept your faults. Accept your mistakes and apologize.

4. Circle in green the words in the grid below that suggest honesty. Circle the words that suggest dishonesty in red. You should be able to find 6 words in all.

5. A good friend is honest. Write only the names of the honest friends from the following in the space provided below.

Sameera loved to paint. She painted all sorts of things, from birds on the trees to the clouds in the sky. The trouble however was that she wasn't good at painting. Her birds never looked like any bird people had seen; her clouds never resembled clouds.

But none of the people around her pointed this out to her. They were sweet to her and always told her that she had painted well.

One day, there was a painting competition. Sameera got ready to participate. The topic was announced five days before the day of the competition. Intending to practice, Sameera painted the Gateway of India. As ever, what she painted did not look like the Gateway of India. Her friends Rita, Sam and Jim did not say so to her. Only Shashi, a new girl in the class, told her so. She also showed Sameera how to draw and paint the Gateway of India.

Sameera's true friends were:

_____   _____

_____   _____

Tips to Parents and Teachers

1.	Do you lie?	Yes, all the time	Yes, sometimes	No, never
2.	Have you ever cheated your friends in a game?	Yes, many times	Yes, sometimes	No, never
3.	Did you ever go to school without completing your homework?	Yes, many times	Yes, sometimes	No, never

You have to be a judge of yourself. Only you can now say whether you are an honest person or not. If your answers are all true, then you are an honest person. If you have lied while answering, you are a dishonest person.

Tips to Parents and Teachers

Rather than be harsh with kids, treat them in a gentle manner and encourage them to tell the truth at all times, and be honest too. For instance, even when the parent knows that the child has done something wrong, rather than threaten them or punish them, they should encourage the child to rectify the mistake. Also, a gentle counseling would work wonders in making the child honest.

Honesty has to become a habit. And developing habits takes time. The earlier children start in life, the better and easier it is for them.

Remember to tell them that you appreciate honesty in them.

Do's and Don'ts

1. Even if you think a lie could save you, you should never lie.
2. Cheating others is a form of cheating yourself. Be honest and don't cheat.
3. Never take what is not yours.
4. Do all your work to the fullest of your abilities.

Respect for the Elderly

We are taught to respect everyone. But respecting the elderly is very important because they are old and wise because of their age.
Being kind to them, hearing them out and helping them in any way we can are ways of showing respect to the old.

Let us read a story from Germany to know more about respecting the old.

The Story

There was once a man called Schmuel. He lived with his wife, son and aged father. The father being old, was slow in his work. He couldn't see well, walk well or even hold things well because his fingers kept trembling.

As a result of this, the old man often spilt his soup on the table. The table-cloth kept getting dirty. Sometimes, the bowl from which he drank his soup also fell and broke. The poor old man tried not to spill his soup or drop his cup, but he couldn't help it.

Now Schmuel was not happy about this. He did not like his table-cloth getting dirty; he did not like losing more pieces of porcelain because of his father. He carved a wooden bowl and gave it to his father. He said, "Father, from now on you will drink your soup from this cup. It is a wooden bowl and will not break."

The old man drank his soup from the wooden bowl. Though he still dropped the bowl at times, it no longer broke like the earlier porcelain ones. But his trembling fingers continued to drop the soup and dirty the table-cloth.

Finally, his son lost his patience. "You will not eat at the table from now on. You will eat in the balcony or in the garden, but not with us," he told his father.

The poor old man felt humiliated. Yet, he went to eat away from the table, where the rest of his family sat to eat.

One day, Schmuel saw his son carving a bowl. He also noticed that there was another chair next to where his father usually sat to eat his dinner. Schmuel asked his son what he was doing.

The little boy replied, "Father, some day you will also grow old and start behaving like grandpa. You too will drop your bowl and break it. So I am carving a bowl for you to use when you become old. The other chair where grandpa sits is for you. I will not want you dirtying my table when I sit for dinner with my wife and children."

Schmuel was shocked. He realized that someday, he too would be old and then he too would be weak and helpless. He did not want to be made to sit away from his family while they had dinner. He realized his mistake. He made his father sit with him for dinner. He helped his father but never got irritated with him again for being weak in his old age.

Have you understood the story? Now answer the following questions.

1. Why couldn't the old man hold things well?
   _____
   _____

2. Why did Schmuel get irritated with his father?
   _____
   _____

3. Why did Schmuel ask his father not to sit at the table for dinner?
   _____
   _____

4. For whom was the little boy carving the bowl?
   _____
   _____

5. What did Schmuel eventually realize?
   _____
   _____
   _____
   _____

More about the Value

The aged in our family were once young. Is it tough to imagine your grandparents as children and young people? Remember that they spent a lot of their lives in raising your parents. They spent their time loving you and your parents; they worked hard to provide for you. In their old age, when they need help and love, you should be there for them. You should speak kindly to the aged. You should not say that you are bored of their company. You should offer any kind of help they require. You should be patient and loving towards them. Above all, you should respect them.

A VALUE FOR ME
Respect your elders; be a better listener than a talker.

Interesting Fact

A book written about 750 years ago is still quite popular in China. It contains 24 stories, all about respecting the aged. The book has been read by many in all these 750 years and it continues to be a favourite among many.

Snippet

There is a story in the Indian epics about the dedication of a young boy towards his aged parents. Sravana Kumar had very old parents. Both his mother and father were old, weak and blind. When they wished to go on a pilgrimage, without hesitating or telling them that it would be very difficult for them to travel, he agreed to take them.

In those days, travel ling to places was difficult. People travelled on foot or by palanquins. But the poor could not afford a palanquin because they also had to hire people to carry the palanquins. And the poor could not pay the palanquin bearers.

Sravana Kumar, however, carried his parents in baskets all by himself.

Let Us Do

1. From memory, fill up the following table as much as you can. Find out the answers to those that you do not know.

Your paternal grandfather's birthday:	Your paternal grandmother's birthday:	Your maternal grandfather's birthday:	Your maternal grandmother's birthday:
What does your paternal grandfather like to eat?	What does your paternal grandmother like to eat?	What does your maternal grandfather like to eat?	What does your maternal grandmother like to eat?
What does your paternal grandfather like to do the most?	What does your paternal grandmother like to do the most?	What does your maternal grandfather like to do the most?	What does your maternal grandmother like to do the most?

What is your best memory of the time spent with your paternal grandfather?	When was the last time you spoke to your paternal grandmother?	When was the last time you did something for your maternal grandfather?	How did you help your maternal grandmother when you met her last?

2. Which of the following statements are true? Write 'true' or 'false'.

a. We should respect the old. _____

b. We should respect only the old in our family and not any other old person. _____

c. We should respect the old because they are weak and helpless. _____

d. The old should be respected because they are wise. _____

e. Even if we don't like some old person, we should respect them and never be rude to them. _____

3. Match the groups of words in the two columns to make complete sentences. They are all ways in which you can show respect to the old.

a. When in a bus or a train	i. to help them walk.
b. Never argue	ii. to cross the street.
c. When any elder person (not just an old person) is talking	iii. or quarrel with an old person.
d. Help old people	iv. give your seat to any old person who is standing.
e. When getting into the car with an old person	v. to go through.
f. Hold the door open for an old person	vi. ask them where they would like to sit.
g. Hold the hands of an old person	v. everyone should be silent and listen.

19

4. **Ask your grandparents about some interesting story from their life when they were your age. You can take ideas from the following:**

  a. How they travelled to school when they were your age.
  b. What games they played.
  c. How they spent their holidays.
  d. The first time they saw a television.

  Write down what you have learnt and share it with your classmates. You can also illustrate to explain what you have heard.

  _____
  _____
  _____
  _____
  _____
  _____
  _____
  _____

5. Make a list of old people you know or like. Also, mention why you like them.

Some old people I know	Why I like them
1.	
2.	
3.	
4.	
5.	

Do you respect the old?

1. Do you like spending time with your grandparents?
2. Do you bring them water or their reading glasses when they ask you to?
3. Do you listen to them when they talk to you?
4. Do you let them watch their favourite programme on TV?
5. Do you insist on making them hand over the TV remote to you so that you can watch your favourite cartoon?
6. Do you wish your grandparents on their birthdays and on festivals?

If your answers to all the questions except the 5th are 'yes', then you respect the old.

Tips to Parents and Teachers

Some Indian customs automatically instill among the children, respect for their elders. For instance, in some communities in India, people touch the feet of their elders on seeing them. This is a mark of respect. Also, children are taught to listen to the head of the family, just as everyone else in the family does.

Such customs help children to understand that the elders and the old are not only respected but that they also have an important place in the family.

Do's and Don'ts

Here are some guidelines on how you can show respect to the old.

1. Spend as many holidays with your grandparents as possible.

2. Wish your grandparents, great uncles and great aunts on their birthday. Make them cards or take a cake to their house on their birthdays.
3. Teach your grandparents how to use the internet.

4. Talk to your grandparents over the phone or through the Internet.
5. Listen to all that your grandparents have to tell you. You can learn a lot through their stories and experiences.
6. Do any kind of work that you can for them. For instance, you can bring them water, or fold up their newspaper after they have read it.
7. Never ever say that you are bored of their company.

Sincerity

Sincerity is the quality of doing things without any intention of cheating the other person. It is the quality of doing something with all your effort. It is the quality of doing something truthfully.

When you do things with sincerity, you not only feel happy, but you are also likely to achieve your goal.

The Story

A long time ago, there lived a girl called Heidi. She was a sweet little girl from a small village in the Alps. Her parents were dead and she stayed with her grandfather in a lonely hut on top of the Alps. Her day started with waking up at the crack of dawn and drinking a cup of fresh goat's milk that her grandfather gave her, straight from the goats.

She and her friend Peter, a goatherd, spent all their time playing on the mountains, while the goats grazed. Heidi loved running about the mountains, with her feet in the soft green grass.

While life looked like a fun time for her, one fine day, Heidi was taken away by her aunt to Frankfurt, a huge city. A wealthy gentleman was looking for a girl to be his daughter's companion. Heidi's aunt thought that Heidi was perfect for this role. She could live in the city, and learn to read and write.

But Heidi found the ways of the city quite strange. Earlier, in her grandfather's hut, she woke up with the sun streaming into her window. She could run straight out onto the mountains. But in Frankfurt, the door of the house she lived in opened onto a busy street. There was no fresh stream of water to drink from, and there was no soft green grass to play on. She was puzzled by the life in the city.

One day, Heidi was asked to bring in a glass of fresh water for a visitor. Now Heidi did not know what to do. She was asked to bring fresh water. But the water from the taps of the city house was not fresh. Fresh water could only be found in a flowing stream.

So Heidi head out of the house in search of a stream. She walked for a long time but she still could not spot a stream anywhere. She asked many people on the way for a stream, but no one bothered to reply.

After a long walk, she finally found a fountain. There was fresh water spurting out of it. This should do, she thought. And so she filled up her glass with the fresh water and headed back home.

In the meantime, the people at home started to worry. They wondered what took Heidi such a long time to fetch some water from the kitchen. When the butler opened the door to see Heidi walk in with a glass of water, the whole household realized what had happened.

Heidi had gone out in a sincere search for fresh water.

Have you understood the story? Answer the following questions.

1. Who was Heidi?
   _____
   _____

2. Why do you think Heidi drank milk that was brought straight from the goats?
   _____
   _____

3. Where was Heidi taken to from her home in the Alps?
   _____
   _____

4. How different was life in the city from that in the village?
   _____
   _____

5. Why did Heidi go out in search of water? Why did she not bring it from the tap in the kitchen?
   _____
   _____

More about the Value

Sincerity is being real. This means that a sincere person will always speak what he feels. He will not lie to please others. He will not lie to save himself from trouble. Also, a sincere person is not afraid of speaking the truth.

Sincerity wins friends. Everyone likes a person who speaks the truth. Everyone likes a person who does and says what he thinks. Hence, sincerity pays.

Also, teachers like sincere students. When children do the tasks elders ask them to do, when children do their tasks without being reminded to do so and when they do their tasks sincerely, they gain the trust and win the love of others.

Though you may end up losing some friends by being sincere, it is for the best not to have such friends. On the other hand, your sincerity will win you good friends who can appreciate the good in you.

A VALUE FOR ME

It pays to be sincere.

Snippet

Long ago, in the schools of the United States of America, children were asked to do manual work in their schools, as a help or as a punishment. There was once a boy who was asked to clean the desks in his school. He had to do it after school hours, when all the children had gone away.

He started cleaning the desks. One by one, everyone in the school had left. There was hardly anyone around to see whether he was cleaning the desks or not. However, the young boy did not skip his work. He meticulously cleaned every desk he was supposed to.

Only when his assigned work was over did he go home. The next day, one of his teachers observed that the boy had done his task very well. He commended the little boy for his sincerity. He told the boy that if he continued to work as sincerely as he did that day, he would succeed in life.

That little boy grew up to become one of the Presidents of the United States of America.

Let Us Do

1. **Fill in the blanks choosing words from the box.**

   > Think   Friends   Pretence   Truthfully   Lie

   a. Sincerity is the quality of doing things _____.
   b. Sincere people never _____.
   c. Sincere people say what they _____.
   d. _____ is the opposite of sincerity.
   e. Sincerity wins good _____.

2. **Who among the following are sincere people?**

   a. Gaurav has some homework to do. He finishes his work and then goes to play.
   b. Sam, Gaurav's classmate, wants to play. He does not do his homework. The next day, he lies to the teacher. He tells her that he had to visit his grandparents and so could not complete his homework.
   c. Pooja, a girl from Gaurav's class, did not know the answers to the mathematical problems in the homework. She asked Gaurav for his notebook and copied the answers from his book.

d. Lalitha, another girl from the same class, also did not know how to solve the mathematical problems. She went to the teacher and said, "Mam, I did not do the homework because I did not know how to solve the problems. Could you explain them again today?"

Who among the above were sincere and who were insincere?

Sincere Children	Insincere Children

3. What should you do?

a. You found a packet of wafers on the park bench. You were hungry, so you ate the wafers in the packet. After a while, a boy came looking for the same packet of wafers. He had forgotten it on the park bench. What should you do?

　i. Remain silent and let the boy keep searching. ☐

　ii. Tell him that you had eaten the wafers and apologize. If possible, you should also buy him another packet of wafers. ☐

b. Your friend's dress is dirty. But she doesn't realize it. What should you do?

　i. Point out to your friend that her dress is dirty and that she ought to go home to change it. ☐

　ii. Let her be and not tell her that her dress is dirty. ☐

c. Your teacher asks you to write a few lines on sincerity. What should you do?

　i. Read about sincerity and write what you understood in your own words. ☐

　ii. Ask your mother or father to write it out for you. ☐

4. Create your own stories using the keywords provided below. You can choose either of the two options, or you can use both the options together to create your own story. Give your story a title too.

   a. Sincere – boy – school

   b. pretend – girl – stomach ache

   _____
   _____
   _____
   _____
   _____
   _____
   _____
   _____
   _____

5. Let us pretend we are interviewing for the school magazine. Work in pairs. Each of you can take turns to interview the other. Remember to jot down the answers, and be sincere in your answers.

   a. What is your name?

   _____

   b. Do you have a pet name?

   _____

c. What is it?

_____

d. What language do you speak at home?

_____

e. Do you have a pet?

_____

f. What do you call it?

_____

g. What is your favourite activity?

_____

h. What is your favourite food?

_____

i. If your father asks you to help, do you help him?

_____

j. If you don't help him, what excuse do you give?

_____

k. Do you ever lie?

_____

l. Do you think you are a sincere child?

_____

Are you a sincere person?

1. Do you lie?

_____

2. Do you feel good or bad when you lie?

_____

3. When someone asks you to do something, do you do it? Or, do you find excuses for not doing it?
   _____

4. When you have to do something, do you do it in the best way you can? Or, do you just think about how to finish the task quickly, not bothering whether you are doing it well or not.
   _____

Lying, not doing the work you are supposed to do and not doing things to the fullest of your abilities are signs of insincerity.

Tips to Parents and Teachers

Being sincere is tough. Insincerity is easier. However, children should not be allowed a chance for insincerity. Monitor the work that the children have to do. Check whether they have completed it or not. Rather than reprimand or punish them for insincerity, instill confidence and positivity in them. This will help them become sincere. They need an incentive to finish their work or to do it well.

Likewise, lying can become an easy habit. Children should be taught to tell the truth no matter what. Rather than punish them for lying, an atmosphere has to be created where they can speak the truth. Most often, children lie when they are scared, or when they don't get what they want. By assuring them that they need not be afraid or that they need not lie for something that they need, one can coax children to develop the habit of speaking the truth at all times.

Do's and Don'ts

1. Say things that you believe in.

2. Don't lie to make others happy.

3. Do only those things that are good and make you happy.

Moral Crossword

With the help of the clues, solve the following crossword.

Across:

2. A stitch in time saves _____.
4. Love for one's country is called _____.
6. A friend in _____ is a friend indeed.
7. _____ is the best policy.
10. _____ is next to Godliness.
13. No act of _____ is ever wasted.
14. Health is _____.

Down:

1. The opposite of truth is _____.
3. Plant more _____. They are our friends.
5. When someone helps you, you should say _____.
8. As far as possible, we should do our work by _____.
9. It is our duty to take care of our health. For this we have to eat a balanced _____.
11. We should be kind to people and to _____.
12. In our country, we speak different _____ and yet we are all Indians.
15. If a lie is bad, then _____ is good.

Non-Violence

When you have a problem with someone, you can either fight it out or talk peacefully and arrive at a solution.

Fighting is violent. Talking peacefully and finding a solution is not violent.

Non-violence is arriving at solutions through peaceful methods.

Let us read a story to know more about non-violence and the need to be non-violent.

The Story

During our freedom struggle, many of our leaders were put in jail.

Once, while Gandhiji was put in the Yervada jail in Pune, another freedom fighter, Sardar Vallabhbhai, Patel was also in there. They both discussed many issues.

Here is an interesting conversation between the two of them:

Gandhiji: A dead snake can also be useful at times.

Patelji: How is that so?

Gandhiji: An old woman once saw a poisonous snake enter her house. She got scared and shouted for help. Her neighbours and passersby heard her and rushed in to help. They managed to kill the snake. One of the men then flung the dead snake onto a ground nearby. A little

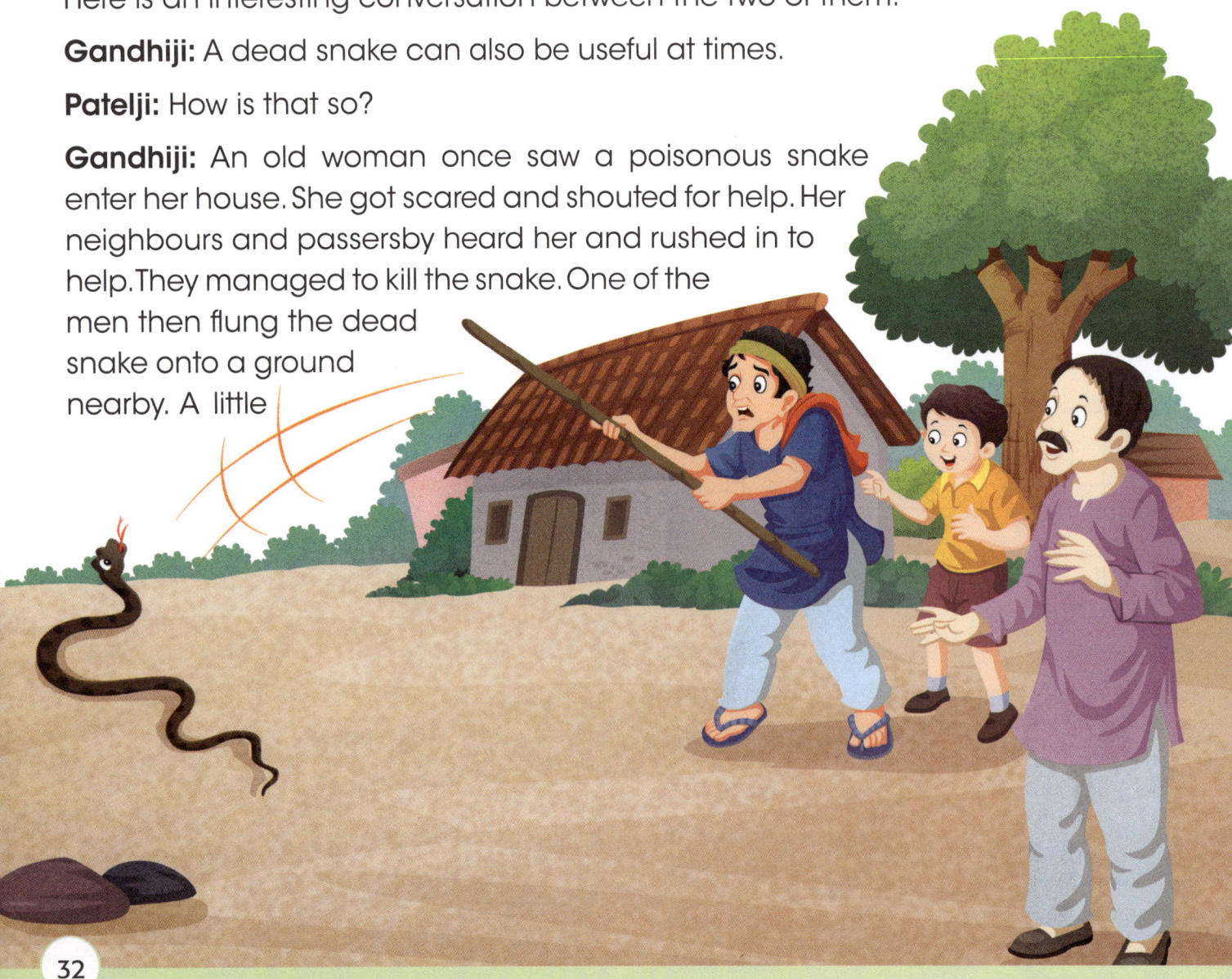

while later, a kite saw the snake, and swooped down to eat it. This bird had an expensive necklace in its beak. To pick up the dead snake, it dropped the necklace. Later, the old woman noticed the necklace and picked it up; she was happy to have found an expensive piece of jewellery.

Patelji: I will now tell you a story. Once, a man found a snake in his house. He didn't like killing creatures even if they were dangerous. So killing the snake was out of question. He wanted to push the snake out of his home. But he wasn't brave enough to do so by himself. There was no one in his house at that time to help him push the snake out. So he inverted a huge pot and put it on top of the snake.

That very night, some thieves broke into this man's house. When they saw the overturned pot, they thought that something valuable was hidden underneath it. One of them lifted the pot and the snake bit him hard. Writhing in pain, he shouted and the man was immediately alerted of the thieves. He bolted himself in his room, safe from the thieves and shouted for help. The neighbours came in and the thieves were caught.

The snake had escaped in this chaos.

Gandhiji: I get your point. A snake needn't be dead for us to be safe; it is not necessary for us to kill something or harm it for us to be safe. We can be peaceful, non-violent and yet be safe.

Have you understood the story? Now answer the following questions.

1. "A dead snake can also be useful at times." These lines were spoken by Gandhiji. True or false?
   _____

2. What had the old woman found near her home, where the dead snake was thrown away?
   _____
   _____

3. In Patelji's story, why did the man not kill the snake?
   _____
   _____

4. Who lifted the pot under which the snake was kept?
   _____
   _____

5. How do you think this story teaches us about non-violence?
   _____
   _____
   _____
   _____

More about the Value

News is filled with violence in the form of wars, murders and fights. Wouldn't we all be happier in a world without these? Violence happens because people do not understand each other; because they are greedy and selfish. If we can curb our desires and learn to tolerate and appreciate others, we can avoid violence. Also, if we learn to share, care and give, we can avoid violence.

A VALUE FOR ME
An eye for an eye will make the world blind.

Snippet

A young boy lived with his parents near Dublin in Africa. His home was far from the nearest city. Once, he and his father had to go to town for some work. The father and son gave their car to be serviced at the workshop. Then the father asked his son to pick up the car in the evening at 4 and pick him up for a particular street.

The boy came across a movie poster while walking through the town. He got tempted and walked into the hall to watch the movie. He forgot all about picking up his car from the workshop. By the time the movie got over, it was quite late. His hurriedly went to the workshop, collected his car and then went to pick up his father.

He lied to his father that the mechanic took time to fix the car. The father realized that the son was lying. He told so to his son and then started walking home. After watching his father walk home for such a long distance, the boy felt miserable. He asked his father why he had walked rather than punish the son.

The father replied, "I wanted to know where I went wrong in bringing up my son that he had to lie to me."

The boy never lied to his parents ever again.

Let Us Do

1. **The following are practices that can lead to non-violence. However, you need to first fill up the blanks in the sentences with words from the box.**

   > Shouting   Think   Count   Apology   Happy

   a. An _____ can help you avoid ill feelings and violence.

   b. Hitting and _____ at others are also forms of violence.

   c. When you are a _____ person, you can make others happy.

   d. Whenever you become angry, close your eyes and _____ to ten. This will help you become calm and think clearly.

   e. _____ before you act.

2. **Cross out from the following list things that you feel lead to violence or are suggestive of violence.**

   a. Peaceful talks with neighbouring countries

   b. Children playing with guns and swords

   c. Wrestling and boxing matches

   d. Meditation

e. A football match

f. Bull fighting

g. Poaching of animals like the tiger and the elephant

h. Teasing other children to hurt them

i. Helping others

3. Choose the correct option.

   a. The Indian Independence was achieved mainly through _____ means.

      i. Violent   ii. Non-violent

   b. Gandhiji preached _____.

      i. Himsa   ii. Ahimsa

   c. An eye for an eye will make the world _____.

      i. Blind   ii. Better

   d. Wars are _____.

      i. Violent   ii. The best way to solve a problem

   e. A non-violent person looks for _____.

      i. Peace   ii. Funny things

4. Do a case study on any one of the two people mentioned below. Find out from your school library or from the internet who they were, why they were famous and how they are role models of non-violence.

i. Nelson Mandela

ii. Martin Luther King

5. When you do not agree with someone, you can tell them so. Sometimes, however, you need to protest to do so. From among the following, pick the methods by which you can protest in a non-violent manner. Circle your answers.

Are you a non-violent person?

1. Do you like to watch violence on TV?
2. Do you enjoy teasing others?
3. Do you like to see others suffer?
4. Are you happy when others are unhappy?
5. Does peace bother you?

   *If the answers to the above are all 'yes,' then you are not a non-violent person.

Tips to Parents and Teachers

You can help your children grow up to be non-violent by ensuring they:

1. have good friends; good friends make a child happy. A happy child is almost never violent.
2. learn to think before they act; if the child is able to understand and anticipate the consequences of his or her actions, it will prompt him or her to stay away from all action that might harm others.
3. learn to be considerate with others; it is essential that the child learns empathy and sympathy. When the child is able to understand or feel the suffering of others, the emotions of others, he/she will stay away from violence.

Do's and Don'ts

1. Be calm at all times.
2. If you get angry, count to 10. It will help you calm down.
3. Never resort to hitting or hurting others.
4. When you are unhappy with someone, tell them so calmly.
5. Revenge is not a means to happiness. Learn to forgive rather than take revenge or punish.

Loyalty

Loyalty means showing a strong support to someone. You can be loyal to your family members, your friends and even to your country.

When you are loyal to someone, you will support them, no matter what hardships you may face. You will never lie to them, never talk ill of them or never let them down.

The Story

The Mughal emperor Akbar, along with his mighty army, was on his way to Udaipur. He wanted to capture that city to make it his own.

The Rajput prince Maharana Pratap stood waiting at the hills near the city. He was defending his city from the Mughals. The interesting story about this war is not merely of the brave fight that Maharana Pratap put up, or the fact that the Mughal army managed to drive the Rajputs away, but that there was a loyal horse that saved its rider.

Maharana Pratap was wounded in the war. He had to be taken somewhere away from the battlefield to be safe. His horse Chetak was also wounded when an elephant's tusks tore into one of the horse's legs.

The horse, despite its injury, ran as fast as it could and led the prince far away from the battlefield.

Though the prince could not win the battle of Haldighati that day, he recovered and went ahead to win back most of his land from the Mughals.

Yet another story of loyalty in that same battle was of a soldier who risked death to save the prince. The soldier realized that his prince was injured. He also realized that the prince's horse was injured. The enemy army that was chasing the prince had to be misled somehow.

So this brave soldier snatched the prince's crown and put it on himself. He then rode away in the opposite direction. The enemy soldiers, mistaking the soldier with the prince's crown to be the prince himself, rode after him and killed him.

It was only much later that they realized that the prince had not died that day at the battlefield.

Many a battles have been won because of loyalty of this kind.

Have you understood the story? Now answer the following questions.

1. According to this story, the Mughal Emperor Akbar was defending his city from the Rajputs. True or false?
   _____

2. Why was the prince Maharana Pratap waiting near the hills along with his army?
   _____
   _____

3. Who was Chetak?
   _____
   _____

4. How did Chetak show his loyalty to his prince?
   _____
   _____

5. The story talks of another episode of loyalty. How did the soldier show his loyalty to the prince?
   _____
   _____

More about the Value

Loyalty comes when you deeply respect or love someone. Loyalty starts with being loyal to your family members. You never speak badly about your family. Whatever happens, you help your family members.

Likewise, when you make friends, you never speak badly about them. You don't cheat them.

When it comes to loyalty to your country, you should not do anything that will harm your country or your countrymen. You respect your flag and wherever in the world you go, you behave in such a way that people think well about you and your country. You can also be loyal to a cause. For instance, if you believe in protecting the environment, you will refuse to take plastic bags from shops. You will always carry a cloth bag with you to carry back groceries and other things from shops. When you do that, you show loyalty to the cause.

Loyalty means:

You have cared about something, you still care about it, and you will continue to care about it in the future too.

You are not loyal if you are silent or if you lie to protect your friends and family. If someone you love has done something wrong, you should tell them so. If someone talks bad about someone you love, you should tell them what they said is false and that they ought not to lie so.

A VALUE FOR ME
When you give loyalty, you get it back.

Snippet

A professor in Japan got himself a pet dog in 1924. The professor returned home every evening by train. The dog somehow managed to reach the train station every evening at exactly the same time the professor's train arrived. They would both then walk back home together. This became a routine for the dog and its master.

Sadly, a year later, the professor fell ill and was hospitalized. He never returned home again. He died at the hospital. The dog was not aware of this. It went to the station as usual to greet its master. The professor naturally did not arrive at the station.

The dog went home that night and returned the next evening. Once again, there was no master to greet. The dog was so loyal to its master that though its master did not turn up day after day, month after month, it never missed going to the station to wait for him for the next ten years.

Let Us Do

1. Which of the following statements are true? Tick the correct box.

   a. When you are loyal, people can depend on you. True / False

   b. If you are loyal to a person, you have to support him even if he is wrong. True / False

   c. Loyalty comes with respect and love. True / False

   d. You can be loyal only to people, not to causes. True / False

   d. When you are loyal, you care. True / False

2. **Tick the sentences that show that you are loyal to someone or something.**

   a. You buy your groceries from the same shop every month. ☐

   b. You gossip about your friends. ☐

   c. You never lie to your family. ☐

   d. You salute your country's flag and stand up whenever the national anthem is being played. ☐

   e. You help keep your community clean. You never litter the park and the roads. ☐

3. **Who among the following would you consider loyal?**

   a. Feroze's school decided to clean the road in front of the school as part of the Swachh Bharat mission. The activity was to take place on Sunday. Feroze was one of the many children who turned up for the activity. He had a huge sack and a broom with him. Image of a boy with a huge sack and a broom on the road.

   Feroze is _____.

   i. Loyal   ii. Disloyal

   b. While going home in the school bus, Rehana overheard a few girls talk ill about her best friends Koel. Rehana did not say anything. She kept quiet and listened to them till it was time for her to get off the bus.

   Rehana is _____.

   i. Loyal   ii. Disloyal

4. **When you are loyal, you (circle the correct options):**

   a. are dependable

   b. are helpful

   c. talk bad about those who hate you and your friends

   d. do anything to help

   e. respect someone or something

   f. hate the things or people you are loyal to

   g. are forced to do things that you don't like to do

   h. care

5. Are you a loyal person?

    a. Do you attend your brother's or sister's performances at school?

    b. When you think and talk bad about your country, do you feel ashamed of it?

    c. Do you tell your friend when he or she does something wrong?

    d. Do you draw with a pen or pencil on your school desks? Do you like making them dirty?

    e. Do you switch off the fans and lights in the room when you are the last person to go out of it?

    *If your answers to a, c, and e are 'yes' and b and d are 'no', then you are a loyal person. You are loyal to your family, your friends, your school, and to the cause of environmental protection.

Tips to Parents and Teachers

Children learn about loyalty more by what you say and do. So make sure to talk positively of your family members, friends, teachers and the community. Even though there might be some bad qualities in children, by highlighting the good in them, you will be giving scope for children to show loyalty towards them.

Do's and Don'ts

1. Never talk bad about someone behind their back.

2. Always behave in such a way that people think good about you, your family that has raised you and the country that you belong to.

3. Don't let anyone disrespect your family, friends or country in front of you.

4. Loyalty does not mean that you stick with your friends or family even when you know they are wrong. When you are loyal, it is also your responsibility to let them know what they are doing is wrong.

A Test of Your Values

1. There is a new girl in your class. You make friends with her. What should you do with your other friends?

    a. Introduce them to your new friend

    b. Forget the old friend and stick to your new friend

    c. Invite your new friend to play with all your old friends

2. You are in a foreign country. You are participating in the Olympic Games, representing India. How should you behave?

    a. In a way that you make your country proud

    b. Disrespect the locals of the country and say that you are greater than them because you are an Indian

    c. Show respect to the locals and win their respect too

3. You find a coin on the road. It is not yours. What should you do?

    a. Pick it up and see if it belongs to anyone

    b. If you cannot find its owner, you donate it to the poor or the needy

    c. You buy yourself a chocolate with it

4. Your elderly neighbour lives by herself. What can you do?

   a. Visit her once in a while and ask if she needs something

   b. Do some chores for her like help her watering her plants

   c. Ignore her because she is not your age

5. You are travelling. You are in a new town. The town in very dirty. The garbage is thrown onto the streets. You too have a garbage bag to dispose. What do you do?

   a. Throw it along with the other garbage in the town on the street

   b. Throw it on the outskirts of the town

   c. Wait till you see a proper dustbin and then throw the garbage bag there

6. You have to paint your garden wall. You do not like to do it. What should you do?

   a. Paint it well even though you don't like to do it

   b. Ask someone else to do it for you and then help them in some way you can

   c. Finish the job shabbily and get done with it

Values for You

Be kind to others

Share with your friends

Love your family

Be friendly with neighbours

Talk softly

Don't shout at people

Smile, you look good that way

Obey rules

Love your country